The World of Genetics

Lynn Van Gorp, M.S.

Life Science Readers: The World of Genetics

Publishing Credits

Editorial Director
Dona Herweck Rice

Associate Editor
Joshua BishopRoby

Editor-in-Chief
Sharon Coan, M.S.Ed.

Creative Director
Lee Aucoin

Illustration Manager
Timothy J. Bradley

Publisher
Rachelle Cracchiolo, M.S.Ed.

Science Contributor
Sally Ride Science™

Science Consultants
Thomas R. Ciccone. B.S., M.A.Ed.,
Chino Hills High School
Dr. Ronald Edwards,
DePaul University

Teacher Created Materials
5301 Oceanus Drive
Huntington Beach, CA 92649-1030
http://www.tcmpub.com
ISBN 978-0-7439-0597-8

Reprinted 2013

Table of Contents

The Basics of Genetics

Reproduction

Reproduction is the process of making young. Each species reproduces its own kind. People make people. Dogs make dogs. Trees make trees. Reproduction is needed for species to survive.

There are two forms of reproduction. In **asexual reproduction**, something can reproduce all by itself. It does not need a partner. One parent cell divides. It forms two new cells. The cells are identical to the parent cell. Bacteria cells reproduce asexually. Most plants have the ability to reproduce asexually, too.

In **sexual reproduction,** two organisms work together. Normal human reproduction is one example. Babies receive genetic material from both parents. Special sex cells are involved. They are called sperm and egg cells.

Young horses are called foals. Young meerkats are called pups.

Identical Twins

Humans can have identical twins. Identical twins are a form of both types of reproduction. They occur when a single egg is sexually fertilized. Then it divides asexually. It separates into two embryos. The two embryos develop into two babies. The babies have identical genetic makeup. This makes a set of identical twins.

What Is a Chromosome?

How can we understand why humans are the way we are? We have to look at our cells. We must look at a material found in the center of our cells. This material is our **chromosomes**.

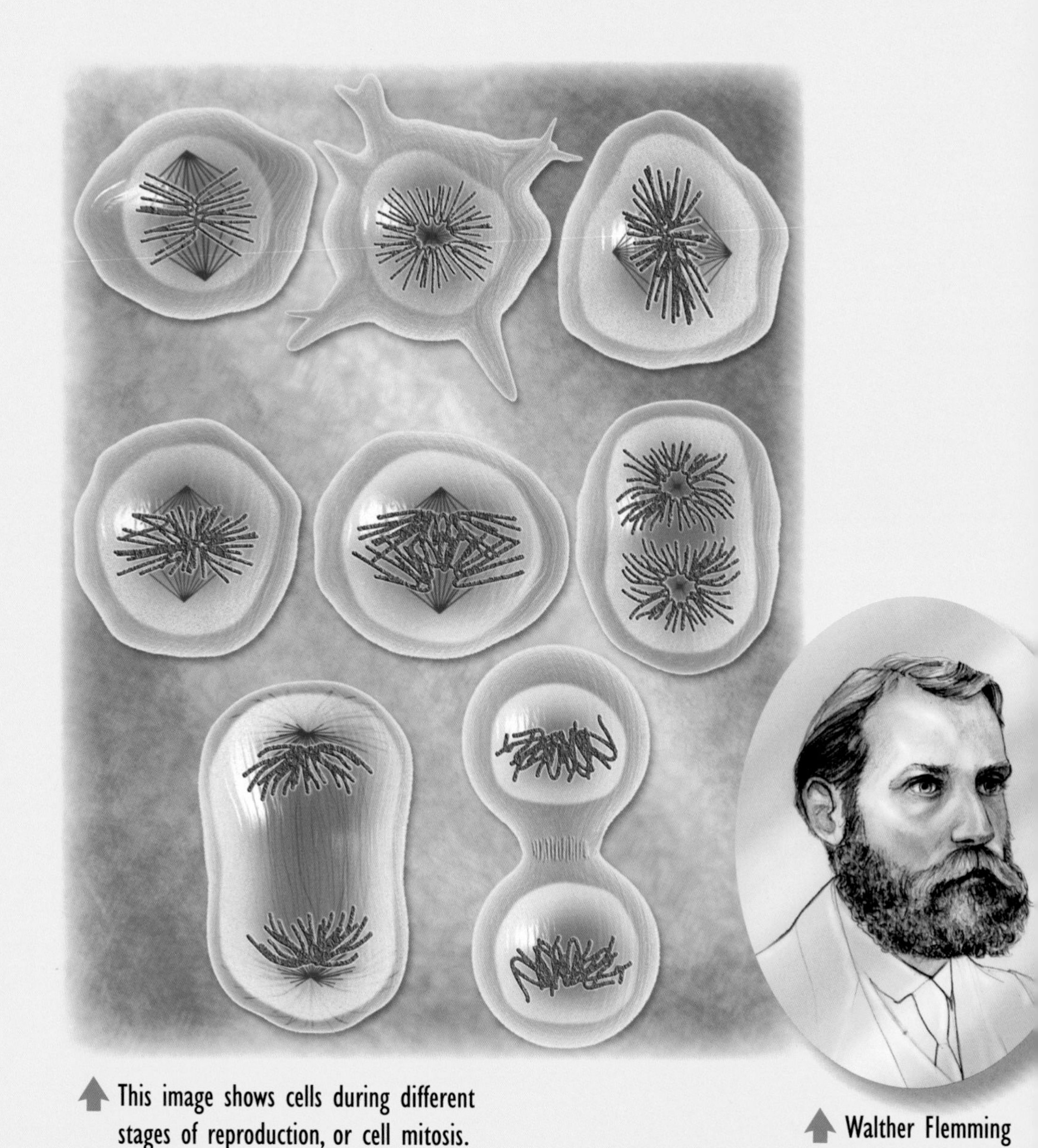

This image shows cells during different stages of reproduction, or cell mitosis.

Walther Flemming

Chromosomes are found in each of our cells. We have 23 pairs of chromosomes. That means each cell has 46 in all. Chromosomes are made up of **alleles**. Each one has more than 2,000 alleles along its length. Alleles are instructions for cells.

Because chromosomes come in pairs, alleles come in pairs, too. Each cell has two sets of instructions for everything. Two paired alleles work together to make a **gene**.

A zebra's genes give it stripes. A bird's genes give it wings. Our genes give us fingers and everything else that makes us human. Stripes, wings, and fingers are all **traits**. Those traits start in the cells. Each cell follows its gene's instructions on how to develop and work. All the cells work together to make stripes or wings or fingers.

Some cells die or are destroyed. New ones are always being formed. This process of cell growth and cell division is called the **cell cycle**.

In 1882, a German named Walther Flemming published a description of cell division. He called it **mitosis**.

Seeing Chromosomes

In 1844, **Karl Nägeli** found a way to see chromosomes better. He found a special stain that made them easier to see. He used a microscope. He looked at cell samples. He was able to see the process of cell growth and division. Try staining onion cells or potato cells with iodine. Then look at them under a microscope to see what **Nägeli** saw.

Potato Chromosomes

Potatoes have more chromosomes than we do! Each plant and animal has a certain number of chromosomes. Humans have 46. Potatoes have 48. The number does not mean how complex an organism is. It's the number of alleles on the chromosomes that does.

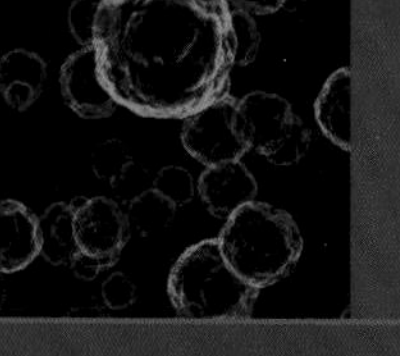

The Cell Cycle

Our bodies need to grow. Our genes give instructions for this growth. Cell growth and division comes in three phases.

The first is **interphase**. It is the period when a cell grows. During this phase, it duplicates the material in the chromosomes. The material is a dense mass inside the cell's nucleus.

centromere

The second phase is **mitosis**. It is a multistage process. The material in the cell's nucleus divides. It forms two nuclei. The first stage is **prophase**. The dense nuclear material condenses into fibers called chromosomes. Each chromosome has two identical strands. These are called **chromatids**. These two strands are pinched together by a **centromere**. This gives the chromosome its *X*-like appearance.

chromatids

The second stage of mitosis is **metaphase**. The chromosomes line up in the center of the cell. The centromere divides. The parts move to opposite ends of the cell.

Next is **anaphase**. The two chromatids separate. They move to opposite ends, too.

The final stage of mitosis is **telophase**. Nuclei form around each chromatid.

The third phase of cell growth is **cytokinesis**. It is the final stage of the cell cycle. The remaining material is distributed between the two cell parts. They finish dividing. The cell division is then complete. Each cell has become two cells. At the end of this phase, each of the two new cells enters the interphase. The cell cycle begins again.

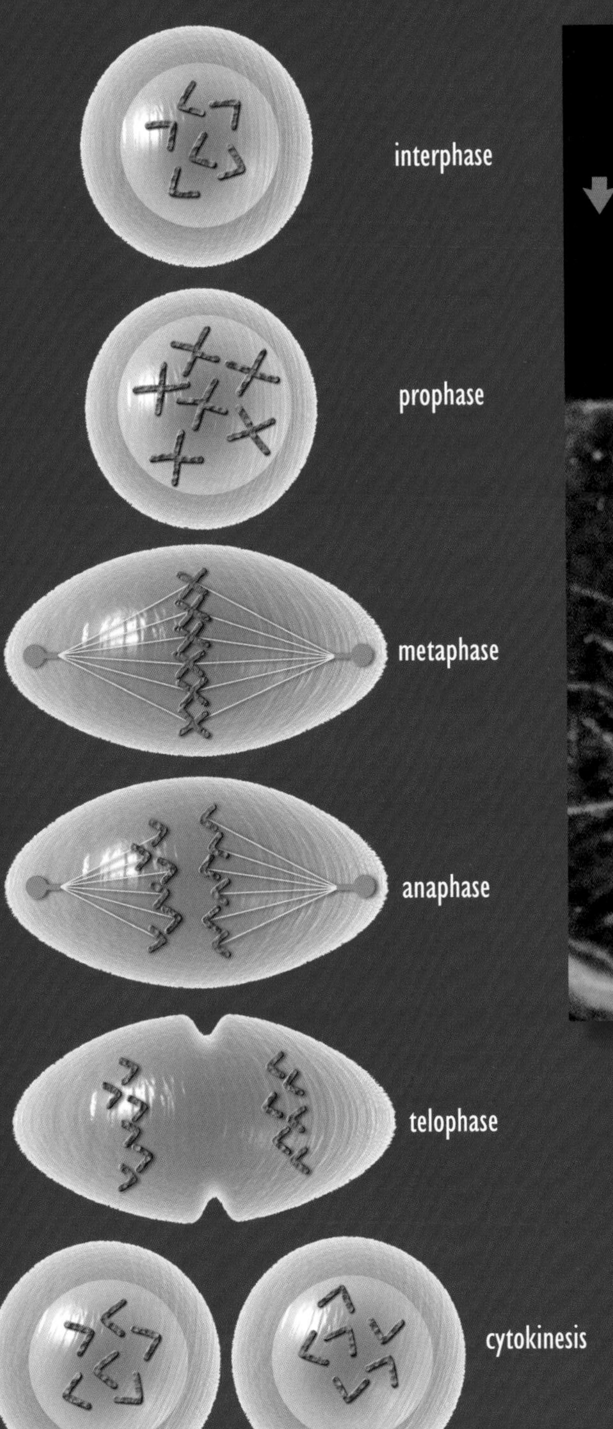

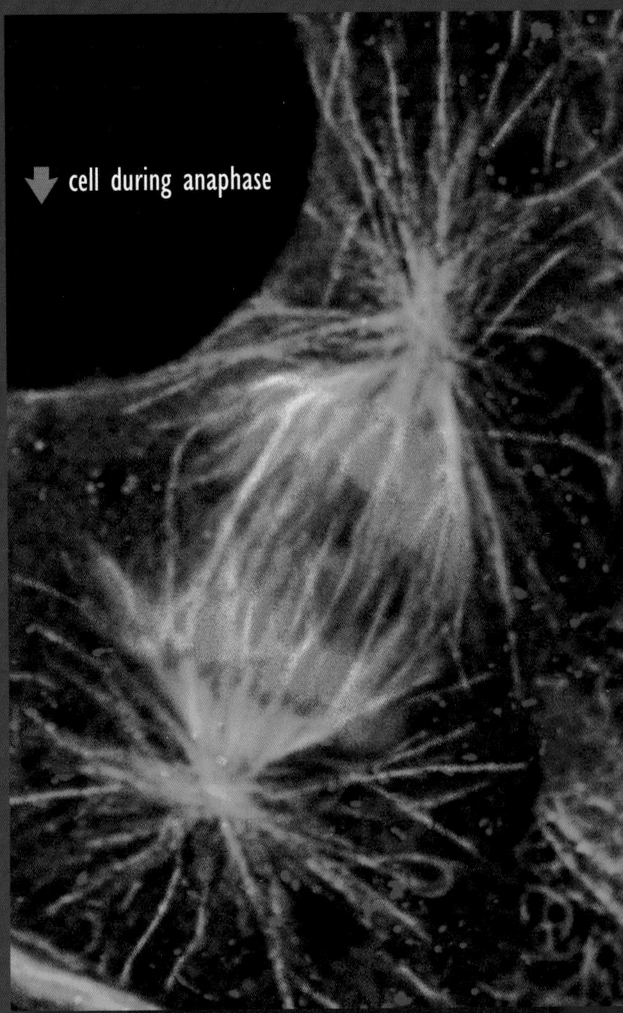

Cell Copies

How long do you think it takes one cell to make a copy of itself? It depends on the cell. The time varies with each organism and cell type. A sea urchin cell takes about two hours to duplicate. A human liver cell takes about 22 hours to duplicate.

Meiosis: Sex Cell Growth and Development

Sex cells are different than body cells. Sex cells are formed during a process called **meiosis**. It is different than mitosis. During mitosis, our 46 chromosomes are duplicated. Two cells, each with 46 chromosomes, are created. In meiosis, a cell duplicates once. Then it divides again. It produces cells with only 23 chromosomes. That is half the usual number.

Males use meiosis to create sperm cells. Females use it to create egg cells. When fertilization occurs, the sperm from the father and the egg from the mother combine. They make one full set of chromosomes. There are 46 chromosomes for the offspring.

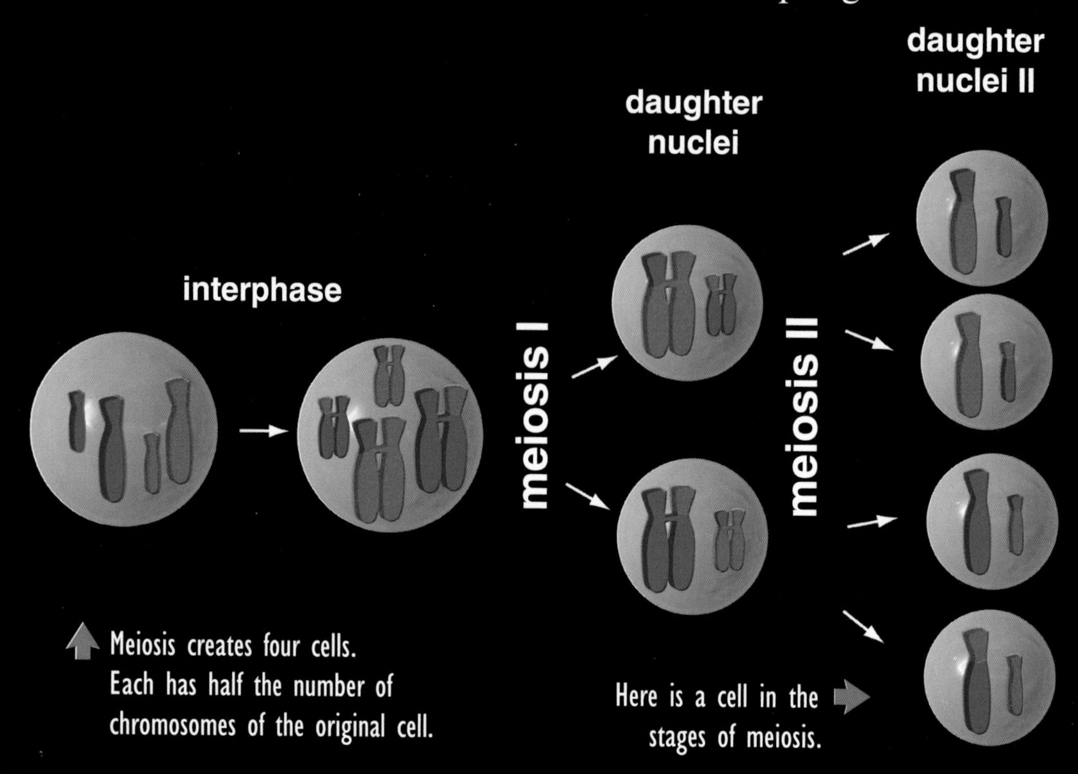

Meiosis creates four cells. Each has half the number of chromosomes of the original cell.

Here is a cell in the stages of meiosis.

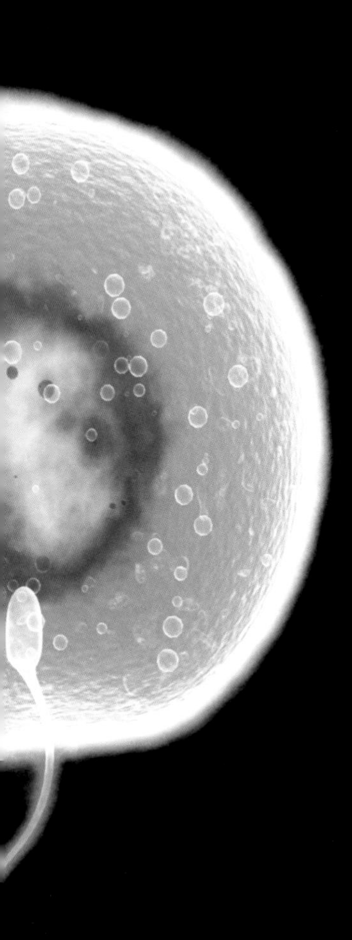

This illustration shows a sperm cell fertilizing an egg cell. Each cell has 23 chromosomes.

Gregor Mendel (1822–1884)

Gregor Johann Mendel is called the father of modern genetics. He was a monk who lived in Europe in what is now called the Czech Republic. He studied many kinds of peas, how they grew, and what made them unique. He learned a great deal about genes and heredity from these plants. Few people were aware of Mendel's work while he was alive. Today, he may be the best-known scientist in this field.

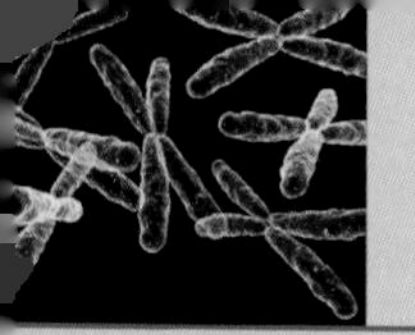

Chromosomes and Inheritance

Sutton

Scientists knew how cells made new cells. They knew that cells followed instructions on the chromosomes. What they didn't know was where a new organism got its instructions from.

A baby's cells worked a lot like its parents' cells. Blonde parents would have blonde children. Whole families would all have the same kind of nose or shoulders. How did they all get similar instructions?

In 1903, Walter Sutton developed a theory. It was the Chromosome Theory of Inheritance. It said that parents pass chromosomes to their offspring.

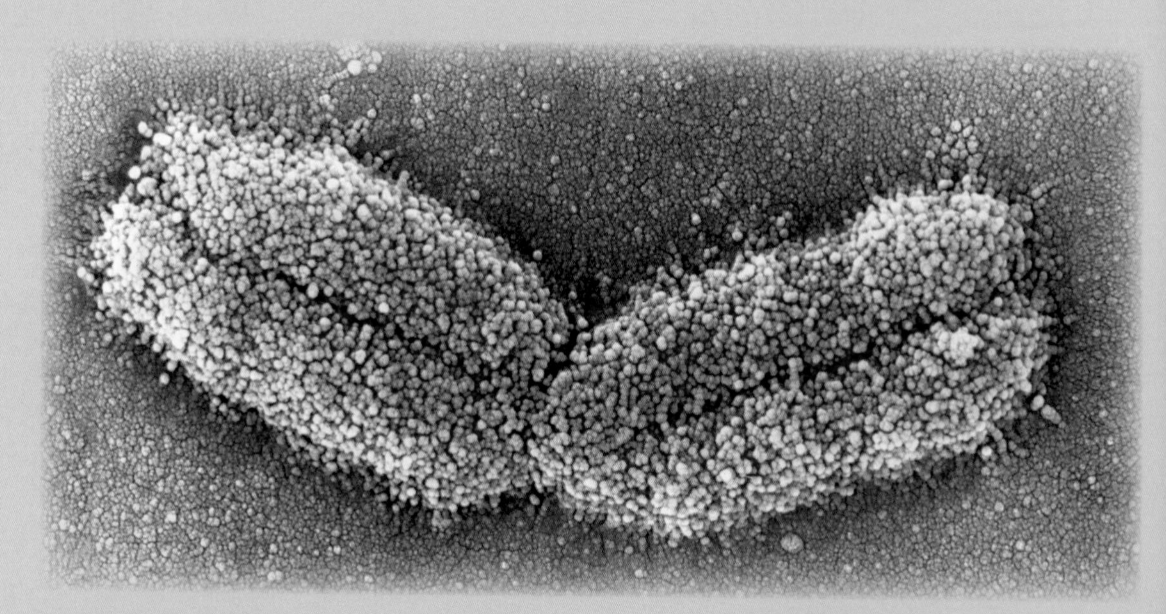

Chromosomes are so small that they can only be seen when they bunch together like this.

A normal cell contains a full set of chromosomes. A full set has 23 pairs. Each pair has one chromosome from the mother and one from the father. If the father was blonde and the mother was blonde, the chromosomes they gave the baby would have blonde alleles. Then the baby would be blonde.

Sometimes the mother and father do not have the same alleles. Then the baby gets chromosomes with different alleles on them. The father's chromosome may have the attached earlobe allele. The mother's chromosome may have the unattached earlobe allele. The baby's cells follow both sets of instructions at the same time. What kind of earlobes will the baby have?

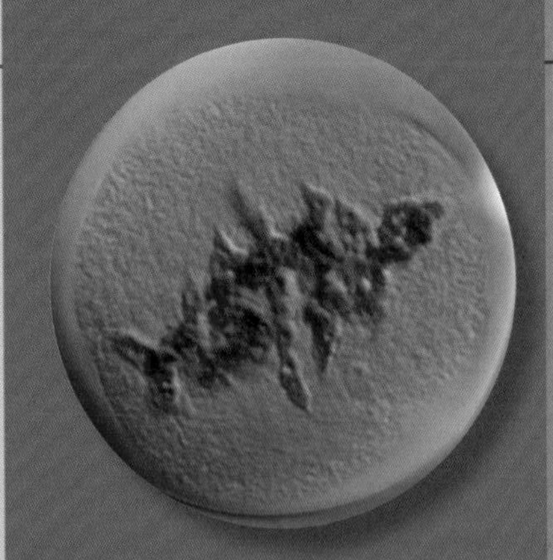

Mixing Chromosomes

During the process of meiosis, the chromosomes can get mixed up. They can recombine in a number of new ways. These new combinations give a variety of genetic possibilities for the offspring.

More About Sutton

Sutton was born in New York. He moved to Kansas when he was 10. He lived on a ranch. He went to college to become an engineer. One summer, though, he took care of his family. They were all very ill. They had typhoid fever. One of his brothers died. At this point, Sutton decided to study biology. He wanted to be a doctor. The world is very glad he did!

You got alleles from both your birth parents. This gave you two sets. Your cells follow both sets of instructions. What happens when the instructions aren't the same?

Some alleles are **dominant**. Others are **recessive**. If a dominant allele is present, that trait will show up. So, if two dominant alleles are present, the dominant trait will show up. When one dominant and one recessive allele are present, the dominant allele will still show up. However, if two recessive alleles are present, the recessive trait will show up.

Alleles are passed down over **generations**. Your mother may have two recessive alleles for attached earlobes. She would have attached earlobes. Your father may have gotten a dominant allele for unattached earlobes and a recessive allele for attached earlobes. He would have unattached earlobes. You would get one of your mother's recessive alleles. You would get one of your father's alleles, too. If you got the dominant allele, you would have unattached earlobes. If you got the recessive allele, you would have attached earlobes.

Black Fur Dominance

With many animals, black fur color is dominant. White is the recessive gene. Most litters of puppies will have many different combinations of alleles. Some will be black and some will be white. It all depends on which combination they got.

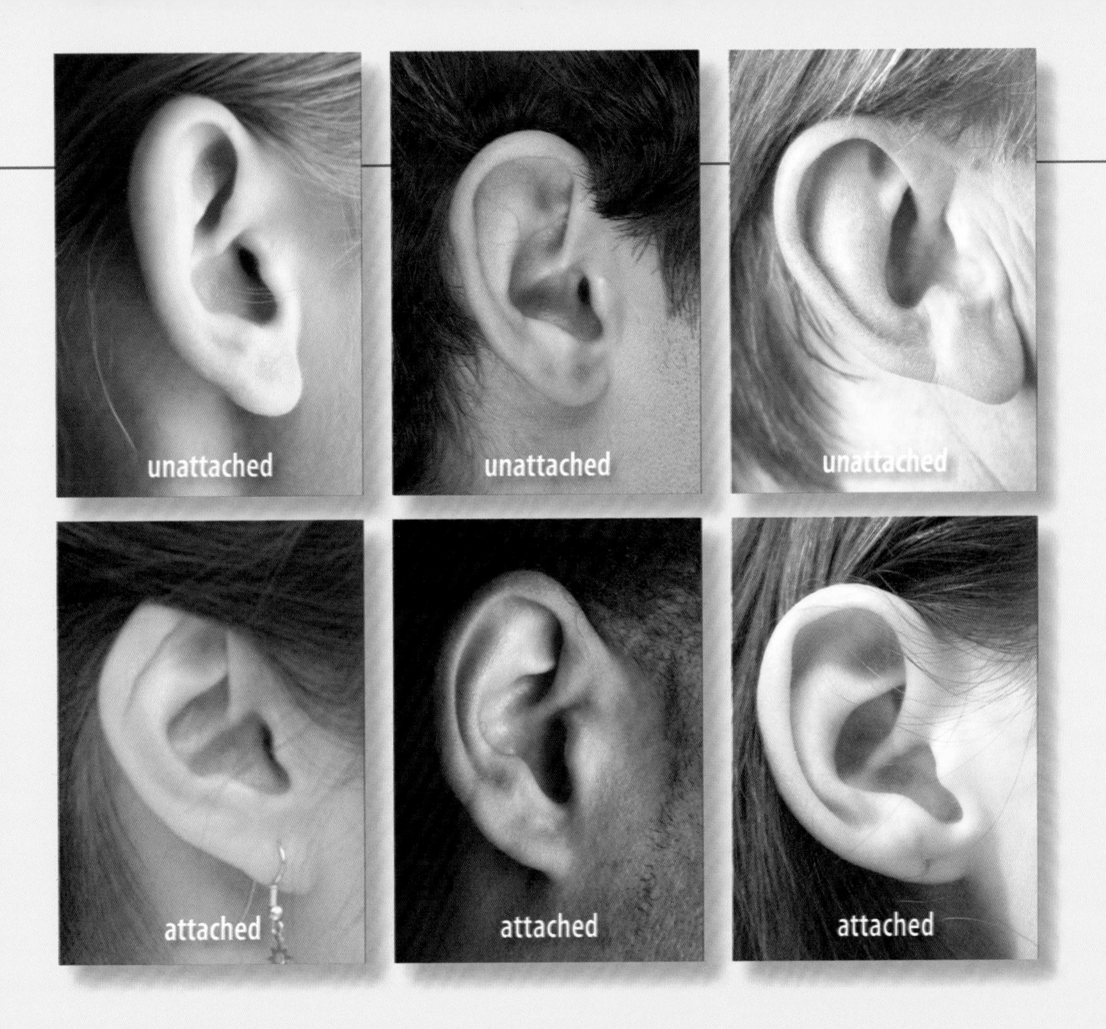

The following chart shows what happens with the earlobe alleles. The gene for unattached earlobes is dominant (*D*). The one for attached earlobes is recessive (*R*). So, to get attached earlobes, you must receive that gene from both your parents.

Mother passes		Father passes		Child has
unattached earlobe (*D*)	+	unattached earlobe (*D*)	=	unattached earlobe (*D*)
unnattached earlobe (*D*)	+	attached earlobe (*R*)	=	unattached earlobe (*D*)
attached earlobe (*R*)	+	attached earlobe (*R*)	=	attached earlobe (*R*)

Punnett Squares and Probabilit

Once scientists knew how dominant and recessive alleles worked, they wanted to map them out. Reginald Punnett developed the Punnett Square. It is a way to diagram allele combinations. It shows the chance of a specific trait appearing.

The Punnett Square below shows the chance that dark or light hair will appear. The mother has a dark allele and a light allele. The father has two light alleles. The mother's egg and the father's sperm will contain only one allele each. So, the mother's egg will have either dark or light. It won't have both alleles. The Punnett Square shows the ways that their alleles could combine in their child.

Interesting Fact

Reginald Punnett and William Bateson helped establish the new science of genetics in 1900. They discovered genetic linkage. Bateson was the first to use the word *genetics*. It came from the Greek word *genno*. Genno means to give birth.

B = dark-hair dominant allele

b = light-hair recessive allele

	Father's allele b	**Father's allele b**
Mother's allele B	Bb	Bb
Mother's allele b	bb	bb

There is a two out of four (50 percent) chance the child will have dark hair. There is a 50 percent chance the child will have light hair.

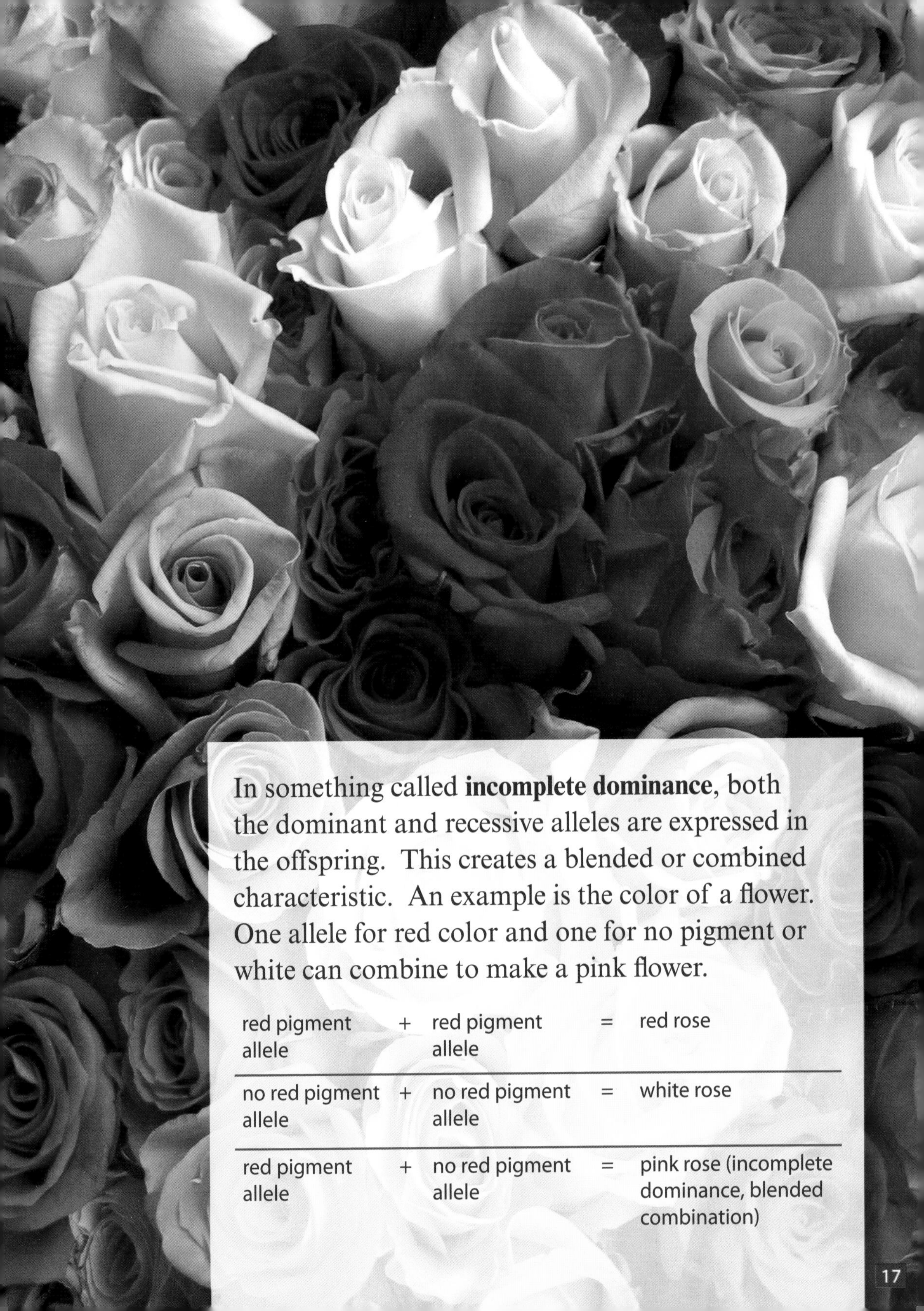

In something called **incomplete dominance**, both the dominant and recessive alleles are expressed in the offspring. This creates a blended or combined characteristic. An example is the color of a flower. One allele for red color and one for no pigment or white can combine to make a pink flower.

red pigment allele	+	red pigment allele	=	red rose
no red pigment allele	+	no red pigment allele	=	white rose
red pigment allele	+	no red pigment allele	=	pink rose (incomplete dominance, blended combination)

Chromosomes: DNA and Protein

In the late 1800s, scientists showed that the nuclei of cells contain chromosomes. Chromosomes are made up of proteins and **DNA**. The scientists believed the proteins carried genetic information. They believed DNA supported the cell reproduction process. Nearly 50 years later, it was proven that DNA, not the protein, carries the genetic information in alleles.

DNA is the blueprint for the cells of an organism. Your DNA tells your body how to put certain materials together to produce certain traits. The DNA molecule is very large. It is shaped like a double helix, or twisted ladder.

a double helix

Twin DNA?

DNA does not change after birth, so twin DNA stays the same. Fingerprints are different. That is because fingerprints are wrinkles from baby fingertips. The fingertips of twins wrinkle in different ways once they're born.

DNA Fun Facts

- DNA is responsible for heredity. It is why many children look like their parents.
- DNA is found in cells that may be left behind in a crime scene. For example, DNA is in blood and hair cells.
- If you stretched out all the DNA in your body, it would be long enough to reach from Earth to the moon 6,000 times!

Most of the time, DNA is just a big mass. It looks like a heap of tangled yarn. It changes when a cell needs to produce more cells. The DNA untangles its mass into the rodlike forms we recognize as chromosomes. Each chromosome holds a very long DNA molecule.

Even the smallest bit of evidence can contain DNA. Police are careful to preserve crime scenes so that every bit of evidence can be found and used to convict criminals.. No one may see the crime being committed, but DNA will tell the tale!

Double Helix

The **double helix** is a double-stranded DNA molecule. Two single strands of DNA spiral around each other. Each strand has its own copy of all the information to make a human being. Having two copies makes it easier for cells to use the DNA. If one is being used, the other can be used at the same time.

It's easier to think of how cells use DNA if you look at a zipper. Think of the double helix coming together and apart. It is like the two sides of a zipper. Imagine the zipper closing and opening. The DNA molecule unzips down the middle of its two strands. Proteins in the cell "read" one or both the strands. The different genes in the strand tell the proteins what to do.

Rosalind Franklin

In the 1950s, Rosalind Franklin produced the first clear photograph of DNA. A couple years later, James D. Watson and Francis Crick used her ideas. They published information about the double-helix structure of DNA. They used Franklin's research and picture of DNA. They won the Nobel Prize for their work.

These students are building a model of a DNA double helix.

Wordy

The longest word in the English language is 1,909 letters long. It refers to a specific part of DNA.

Barbara McClintock (1902–1992)

In 1983, Barbara McClintock won the Nobel Prize for her work in genetic research. She began her work in the 1920s with the study of chromosomes. She went on to become one of the foremost scientists in the field of genetics. She lived to the age of 90, and her career lasted for nearly 70 years!

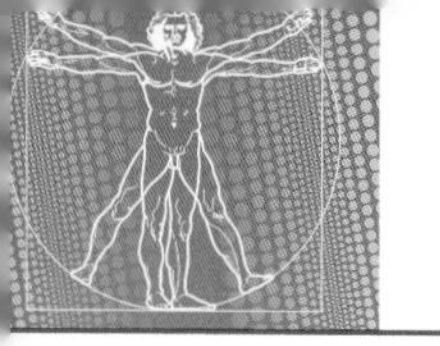

Human Genome Project

In 1990, two agencies in the United States joined together for a common goal. They were the U.S. Department of Energy and the National Institutes of Health. They coordinated the **Human Genome Project**. It turned into a 13-year project. The Wellcome Trust of the United Kingdom was a major partner. Japan, France, Germany, China, and other countries were involved, too.

The Human Genome Project's goals were to:

- identify all the genes in human DNA. There are approximately 20,000–25,000.
- determine the sequences of the chemical base pairs that make up human DNA. There are about 3 billion of them.
- store this information in databases.
- improve tools for gathering the data.
- transfer related technologies to the public.
- address the issues that may arise from the project. This includes the ethical, legal, and social issues.

Wendy Bickmore

Wendy Bickmore is a genetic researcher from the United Kingdom. She conducts research to find where human chromosomes and genes are located in the nuclei of cells. She also studies how their positions affect them.

Update

Ten years later, U.S. President Clinton and U.K. Prime Minister Tony Blair agreed to work together. They believed that the public should have free access to all the Human Genome Project data. They encouraged private companies to invest in gene-based technology. They wanted researchers to use this information. They hoped new medicines would be invented as soon as possible. There was a challenge to learn 90 percent of the sequences of DNA within five years.

Craig Venter was the CEO of Celera, a private company. He had been competing with Francis S. Collins and the Human Genome

Anna Starzinski-Powitz

Anna Starzinski-Powitz is a German research scientist. She works with genetics and the functions of cells. She earned her degrees in the 1970s. It was a time in Germany that did not support women becoming researchers. Even today, people who don't know she is a woman call her Herr Professor. *Herr* is the German word for Mr.

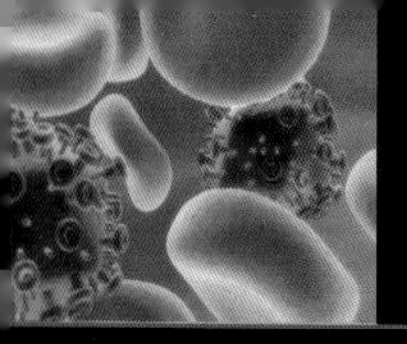

Mutations

Extra Toes

One in 10 cats in New England has six or seven toes on each paw. This is likely due to a cat that came over with the Pilgrims in the 1600s. That cat had extra toes. This trait has been passed on to future generations of cats.

Mutations are changes in genetic information. They can be caused by copying errors during cell division. They can also be caused by exposure to radiation, chemicals, or viruses. They can be a source of beneficial genetic variation. They can also be neutral or harmful in their effect. Some mutations result in offspring having too many chromosomes. Others result in too few. These types of mutations cause some genetic disorders.

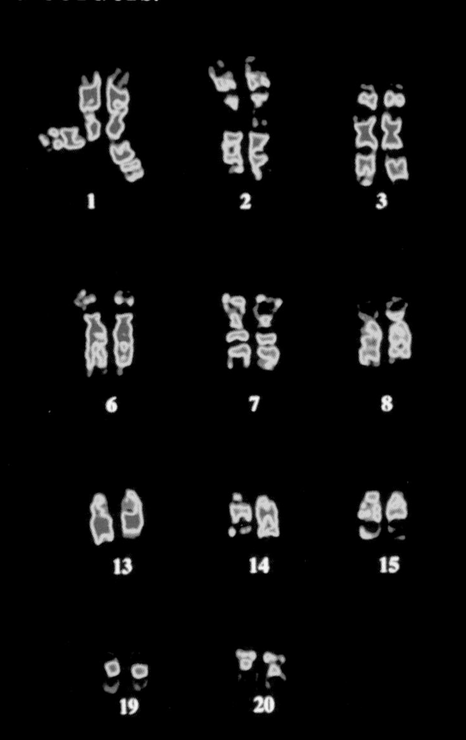

Harmful Mutations

Individuals with Down syndrome have an extra copy of chromosome 21. People with Down syndrome have a distinct physical appearance. They also have some degree of mental retardation.

Cystic fibrosis affects many of the body's organs. Changes in the CFTR gene leads to cystic fibrosis. This disorder causes progressive damage. The respiratory and digestive systems are affected.

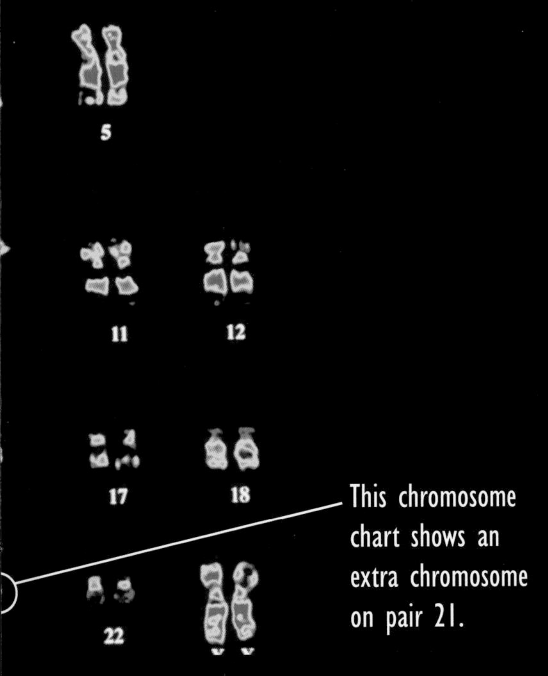

This chromosome chart shows an extra chromosome on pair 21.

Mutations Can Block Disease

Dr. Stephen O'Brien investigated a genetic mutation. It is one that helped people be immune to the **bubonic plague** in the 1300s.

He looked at the mutated CCR5 gene, delta 32. It might have prevented the plague from entering a person's white blood cells. Recent work with **HIV**, the virus that causes **AIDS**, shows that it affects the immune system in a similar way. Drug companies are trying to develop a drug that will copy delta 32. They hope it will block HIV.

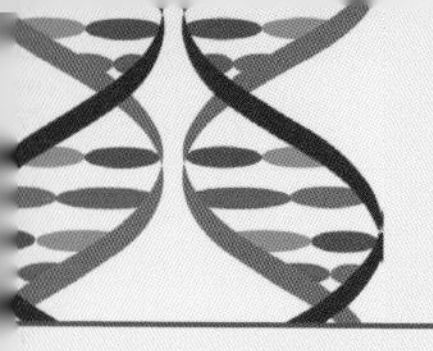

Cloning

Cloning is the process by which an offspring is created with the exact genetic makeup of only one parent. The idea of cloning living beings used to be part of science fiction. In the last century that all changed. The Roslin Institute is a government research institute in Scotland. Scientists there created Dolly. Dolly was a sheep. She was the first mammal to be cloned from an adult cell. After Dolly, goats, pigs, mice, and cows were cloned.

Dolly, the clone sheep, and her firstborn lamb, Bonnie

Could Human Clones Be Next?

Cloning humans is an issue that will require a lot of serious thought. Some people are opposed to cloning for religious reasons. They believe that the scientists would be playing God. Others are afraid that cloning would create a situation such as the one that occurred in Nazi Germany during World War II. A group of people might want to make a "perfect" race. They might want to get rid of people with certain undesirable traits. Another concern is that cloning could reduce variety in the human gene pool. This would be a dangerous thing to do, too. Variety helps to create stronger, healthier people.

Many scientists believe that using cloning would be worthwhile. It could help to prevent disease and abnormal genetic mutations. But most think we should learn more about cloning before we use the process with people. What do you think?

The Trouble with Cloning

It took scientists 227 tries to get Dolly, the cloned sheep. Early clones were seriously deformed. They soon died. The scientists who cloned Dolly don't think humans should be cloned. They think the risks are too high.

The First Clone

The first cloned animal was a tadpole. It was cloned in 1962.

Lab: Genetic Dominant/Recessiv

In this lab, you will survey your families and friends. You will find out how many of them display certain dominant or recessive traits. The trait pairs you will survey are the following:

Dominant	Recessive
free earlobes	attached earlobes
can roll tongue in a *U* shape	can't roll tongue in a *U* shape
no widow's peak	widow's peak
brown eyes	grey, green, or blue eyes
index finger shorter than ring finger	ring finger shorter than index finger
dark hair	light hair
non-red hair	red hair
curly hair	straight hair

Materials

- paper
- pencil
- computer with spreadsheet application and a printer (optional)

Procedure

1 Prepare a genetic dominant/recessive trait survey form. Using each of the categories listed at the top of this page, make a chart. Leave space after each column to tally total numbers. Above the left-hand column, add the title Dominant Traits. Above the right-hand column, add the title Recessive Traits.

Trait Survey

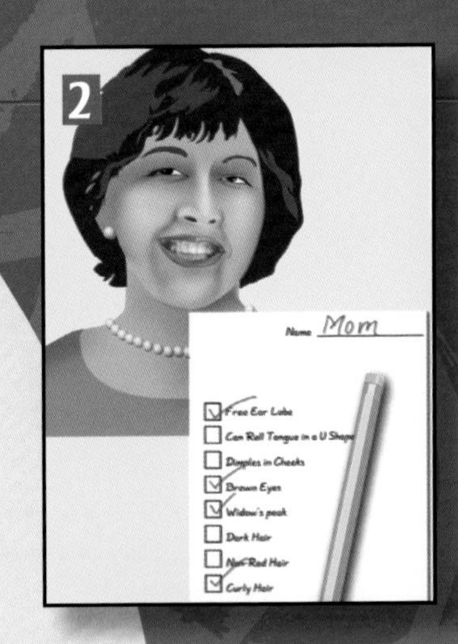

2 Ask your family members and friends which traits they have.

3 Record their responses on your form.

4 Total the number of responses you tallied for each trait.

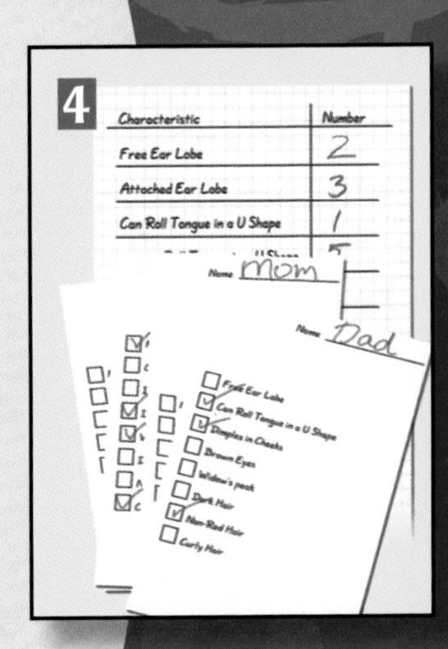

5 Create a bar graph to display your results. If you have them, use a computer and printer to create your graph.

6 Summarize your results.

Conclusion

Dominant traits show up more often than recessive traits. Genetic traits show up in predictable patterns within families. Did you come to the same conclusion?

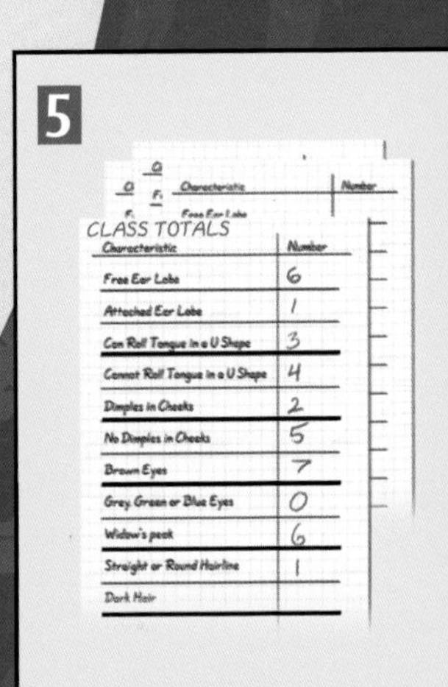

5

CLASS TOTALS

Characteristic	Number
Free Ear Lobe	6
Attached Ear Lobe	1
Can Roll Tongue in a U Shape	3
Cannot Roll Tongue in a U Shape	4
Dimples in Cheeks	2
No Dimples in Cheeks	5
Brown Eyes	7
Grey, Green or Blue Eyes	0
Widow's peak	6
Straight or Round Hairline	1
Dark Hair	

Extension Idea for Further Study

Use genetics as a keyword to research genetic traits on the Internet. Share your most interesting findings by creating a poster.

Glossary

AIDS—a disease of the immune system caused by HIV

alleles—different forms of a gene that control a particular characteristic

anaphase—the last stage of cell division, during which chromosomes move to opposite ends of the nucleus

asexual reproduction—reproduction that involves one parent instead of two

bubonic plague—infectious and usual fatal disease carried by fleas, that killed millions in the 1300s

cell cycle—the process of cell growth, division, and reproduction

centromere—center of a human chromosome where two chromatids are joined to each other

chromosome—rod-shaped structure in a cell's nucleus that carries the genes that determine traits

chromatid—one of the two strands of a chromosome that is visible during the process of cell division

cloning—created offspring with the identical genetic makeup of one parent

cytokinesis—division of the cytoplasm during the cell cycle

DNA—deoxyribonucleic acid

dominant—a gene that, when present, will always cause a particular characteristic to show

double helix—the spiral structure of DNA

gene—located on chromosomes, the basic unit capable of passing traits from parent to offspring

generation—all the offspring at the same stage that descended from a common ancestor

genetics—a branch of biology that involves studying heredity and genetic variations

HIV—human immunodeficiency virus; causes AIDS

Human Genome Project—an international research program that recorded the entire human genetic code

incomplete dominance—both the dominant and recessive gene alleles show, creating a blended or combined characteristic

interphase—phase in the cell cycle in which the cell is resting or growing but not dividing

meiosis—the process of a cell division that makes sex cells that have half the usual number of chromosomes

metaphase—second phase of cell division in which the chromosomes line up to separate

mitosis—cell division that creates two cells with the same number of chromosomes as the parent cell

mutation—a change in a chromosome or gene that results in a new trait

prophase—first phase in cell division in which chromosomes condense and are seen as two chromatids

reproduction—production of young plants and animals through a sexual or asexual process

recessive—a gene that needs a matching gene or allele before its trait shows

sexual reproduction—reproduction involving a male and female, with each contributing half the genetic makeup

telophase—phase of cell division in which a nucleus forms around each chromatid

trait—a genetically determined condition or characteristic

Index

Sally Ride Science

Sally Ride Science™ is an innovative content company dedicated to fueling young people's interests in science. Our publications and programs provide opportunities for students and teachers to explore the captivating world of science—from astrobiology to zoology. We bring science to life and show young people that science is creative, collaborative, fascinating, and fun.

Image Credits

Cover: Kirsty Pargeter/Shutterstock; p.3 Galina Barskaya/Shutterstock; p.4 (top) Cre8tive Images/Shutterstock; p.4 Condor 36/Shutterstock; pp.4–5 EcoPrint/Shutterstock; p.5 (top) Galina Barskaya/Shutterstock; p.5 (bottom) Judy Tan; p.6 (left) Tim Bradley; p.6 Rick Reason; p.7 (right) Rick Reason; p.8 (top) Arbi Babakhanians/Shutterstock; p.8 Cre8tive Images/Shutterstock; p.9 (left) Tim Bradley; p.9 THOMAS DEERINCK, NCMIR/Photo Researchers, Inc.; p.10 Tim Bradley; p.11 (left) CHRISTIAN DARKIN/SCIENCE PHOTO LIBRARY/Photo Researchers, Inc.; p.11 (right) Bettmann/CORBIS; p.12 (top) Sebastian Kaulitzki/Shutterstock; p.12 (left) Rick Reason; p.12 (bottom) ADRIAN T. SUMNER/SPL/Photo Researchers, Inc.; p.13 (left) Justin Horrocks/iStockphoto; p.13 (right) Clouds Hill Imaging Ltd./CORBIS; p.14 Andrey Nikiforov/Shutterstock; p.15 (top row) Photos.com; (bottom left and center) Photos.com; (bottom right) Lara Barrett/Shutterstock; p.16 (top) Fribus Ekaterina/Shutterstock; p.16 Rick Reason; p.17 Christophe Testi/Shutterstock; p.18 (left) Cre8tive Images/Shutterstock; p.18 (right) Brian Erickson/Shutterstock; p.19 Loren Rodgers/Shutterstock; p.20 Charles Gupton/CORBIS; p.21 (left) Science Source; p.21 (right) USPS; p.22 (top) Rzymu/Shutterstock; p.22–23 Rick Reason; p.24 (top) Sebastian Kaulitzki/Shutterstock; p.24 (left) Michael Ventura/Alamy; p24–25 Biophoto Associates/Photo Researchers, Inc.; p.25 (top) Rick Reason; p. 26 (top) iconex/Shutterstock; p.26 P. A. News/CORBIS; p.27 Thomas Mounsey/Shutterstock; p.28 (top) Cre8tive Images/Shutterstock; pp.28–29 Nicolle Rager Fuller